NATURAL OCCURRENCES

(And All Things Thereafter)

Theo Daniel

BookLeaf Publishing

India | USA | UK

Natural Occurrences (And All Things Thereafter) © 2022 Theo Daniel

Presentation by *BookLeaf Publishing*

Web: www.bookleafpub.com

E-mail: info@bookleafpub.com

ISBN: 9789358739206

First edition 2022

Dedicated To

Jordan

My parents: Sal & Liz

Justin & Angel

Little Jameer, Tianna and Olivia

My dear friends, Leah, Rubi and Heather

Colleen (the greatest writing professor to exist)

My team at 1214

The Bookleaf Publishing team for making this a reality

Preface

This book of poetry captures my mind in it's most *dreamlike* state, where my thoughts get away from me and a lone phrase sparks a stream of *creativity*.

My poetry can be inspired by the natural things I see around me at the time of writing, or can be about those things I will never know for sure – and most of my poems tie back to a real feeling or have parallels to the complexities of *relationships* and *existentialism*.

Thank you, for joining me on a journey of self- discovery, wonder and reflection.

The In-Between

I live with ghosts, they haunt me in little ways:

The aroma of their coffee overwhelms me

In their absence during the day.

At night I listen to their return;

Arguments shake through the wall in my room.

My hands tremble as they press against my ears,

I watch a marriage fall to ruin.

I live with ghosts, they convince me:

"It's not your fault," and "we're still friends".

Marriage always leaves one ghost in the end.

Spectre Lake

Ripples in the water;

Ghosts walk on the lake.

Though we don't see them

They linger on the beach where we play.

They watch us,

As we play and make our jokes

They're reminded of the laughter they once had

As they dodge our skipping stones.

They only wish to feel,

The gentle breeze, the sun on their skin.

Still, they go unnoticed,

Longing for life within.

They don't want to scare us,

They don't want us to scream, or fret.

What they want, more than anything,

Is to have a friend.

Celestial

The man in the moon looks blue;

it must be lonely up in space

where craters echo your thoughts,

and distant bodies lie,

in your line of vision

where you may fixate all

your wildest fantasies upon

the dying planets,

the celestial wonders,

you will never experience.

Echoes

Beneath the field of lilies are the bodies of men,

buried besides their women, children and pets.

Listen to their stories, and breathe in their scent.

Revel in their memories as you walk past their stems.

Don't ignore their beauty,

or their whispers which fill the wind.

Their bodies deeply buried,

but histories never forgotten.

Floating

The view from above the clouds,

looks like waves crashing on the beach.

It is all the beautiful chaos

of the small curiosities

you find out at sea

Ouija

"Hello"

A million eyes are on me,

But nobody is near.

A million voices,

They scream into my ear.

A thousand full moons,

Rising to fall.

When darkness sets,

That's when they call.

A hundred doors,

Which one will open next?

And who will I see creeping,

Through the vortex?

Only twenty-six letters,

A 'yes' and a 'no'.

Ten numbers,

A goodbye and hello.

Four white walls,

They draw ever so close.

It's easy to feel crowded,

Amongst a million Ghosts.

"Goodbye,"

Paper Lanterns

Little embers always spiral,

they float away from the fires we create

Small arguments that spark,

embers like ripples in our lives

Catching the wind,

To be transported

Some to extinguish ,

Without interference

Some to spread flame

To all of the dull,

Seemingly safe things we hold so dear.

12

Eclipse

Radiance to darkness:

A smile erased.

Butterflies to bats.

A relationship soon replaced.

Halves in hands:

A heart in two.

Tears in trails,

They bring me back to you.

I entered happy:

Deaf, dumb, blind.

Brought from love,

To a place the sun no longer shines.

Tiger Lily

An explosion of vibrancy as I ascend,

Nobody cares what I hide within.

A mind masked by beautiful colors,

They always choose me over the others.

I stand still as they all watch,

None the least bit concerned with my
thoughts.

They hold me up as a symbol of perfection,

Though I lead a life with no direction.

I live my life, reflected in their eyes.

Their faces astonished by my guise.

Everyone thinks I've had a life well spent,

But would they notice me if I were a leaf
instead?

Storytellers

Give me your memories,

pass your stories down to me

Share with me your experiences,

tell me those dear moments that set you
free.

Let your smiles go unhidden,

and your inhibitions run wild

So that maybe when you're gone,

we can remember you for a little while.

Repression

Skipping stones, our thoughts

They skip across the way.

They always get lost through the day.

Harmless, our games.

We play them nearly every day.

Uncaring that no work comes from play.

How heavy, our traumas,

They bare a certain weight.

Skipping stones that never make it…

Across the lake.

Fireworks

Fireworks; spirits that burn bright

They cross the veil

And cut through the night

They leave behind trails

Bright like fireflies

They pierce the sky

And illuminate eyes

We stand astounded

And watch them soar

Until we can't see

Their lights sparkle, anymore

Tranquility

Serenity exists in natural spaces;

Your head clears with the sun's warmth on
your glowing skin

Your sighs dismiss the white thistles from
the dandelion's stems

The water washes your fears and cleanses
your soul,

So that you are prepared to fight any fires in
your heart

And may one day find the peace to allow
the beautiful earth to accept your body,

whole.

Lavender

Her favorite season is autumn,

She says she loves the change.

Her outer beauty is a mask

It hides her internal pain.

And some might call her unique

Some would call her strange.

Some would say she's different

But reality is, she's the same.

Her mother was a dancer.

Not in videos or ballets.

She'd watch her fans

Throw dollars on the stage.

And mother worked hard

To give baby those things

The life she always wanted

Instead, a young angel with broken wings.

And so Lavender has grown,

With beauty, but not grace.

She makes her living from her body,

All wrapped in black lace.

And she tells all of her friends,

That it's just for fun.

Though she never sees them,

Because the drugs in her veins.

And so she lives every season

Hoping for autumn again.

Through cold winters,

Pleasing business men.

Friends missing from her heart

With drugs filling that empty space.

And through all the years that autumn changes,

Lavender stays the same.

Timeless

How peaceful it must be to be a ghost

No more worries about things to be done

All your responsibility is lost to you

And that burden placed on another no one

No more wondering about time

For you it never runs out

Nothing to do before you die

Just watch the rushing lives of everyone
else

Afloat

Leaping from Lily pads

With your head above water

Peeping through the reeds

Watching for predators

Steering through streams

To find your place

Never to sink

Afloat in everlasting grace

Tug

You pull at my heart:

My emotional harpist.

I wait for the tears to land,

And I listen for your lyrics.

You tune my body,

You wind each chord.

I, a most malleable instrument

Who you use to write your score.

You can pluck at my feelings

Fingers writhe all day.

You can force the beauty of a note,

But I can't be forced to like the melodies
you play

Jordan

Snow on the peaks of my heart

You melt it away

And the butterflies in my stomach

They're here to stay

The fireworks in your eyes

Make the sun shine pale

And the sound of your voice

Makes all my fears frail.

You've shown me the world

Together we explore

As long as I have you,

I'll never need anything more

Disaster

Life is unpredictable

Like wild lightning in an empty field

So suddenly the tranquility could easily be

Disrupted

And all the delicate beauties

That took so long to naturally form

Disintegrated

And as quickly as you can recover

As fast as you may heal

The storm can roll back in to

Devastate

The Presence

If these walls could speak,

Well, they simply do.

Each embedded eye,

Is fixed on you.

You flinch at their voices,

Their calls so faint.

But you don't see your watchers,

As they blend into the paint.

Too scared to look up,

At the man who crawls on the roof.

He smiles in silence,

And absorbs your truths.

If these walls could speak,

You'd beg them to hush.

They'd reveal demons so actualized

They're real enough to touch.

9 789358 739206